A Builder's Life

Dave Hawkes

authorHOUSE®

AuthorHouse™ UK Ltd.
500 Avebury Boulevard
Central Milton Keynes, MK9 2BE
www.authorhouse.co.uk
Phone: 08001974150

© 2009 Dave Hawkes. All rights reserved.

No part of this book may be reproduced, stored in a retrieval system, or transmitted by any means without the written permission of the author.

First published by AuthorHouse 1/30/2009

ISBN: 978-1-4389-5005-1 (sc)

Printed in the United States of America
Bloomington, Indiana

This book is printed on acid-free paper.

INTRODUCTION

Hello and welcome to the world of an ex-boxer and now builder. I hope you enjoy this book.

I am a happily married man with a lovely wife, Sue, and two great children. Our son, Richard, is married to Jaine, our beautiful daughter-in-law, and they have a son, Thomas. Karen, our beautiful daughter, has a daughter, Isabelle. Our children and grandchildren are very precious to us and never far from our thoughts. We have a lovely bungalow near Farnham, and we both work hard—hard enough that it catches up with us in the evenings, and we sleep early, whether we like it or not.

I think it would be true to say that we have worked hard and have been rewarded. I know many men and women who have worked hard all their lives and have very little to show for it, through no fault of their own, just circumstances. I also have a mum who is nearly eighty-seven and now lives in a residential home in Farnham, a brother and his wife, one niece, one nephew, and many cousins and second cousins and their families. Also my sister-in-law on my wife's side but, for all that, we are not a large family. Dad died in 2001 at eighty-two. The last eighteen months of his life were very painful for him. Before that, he had hardly ever seen a doctor.

My wife works very hard; is this true of all women? Apart from running our home with all that entails, she works two to three days a week for an accountant. She does a lot of secretarial, bookkeeping, and accountancy work at home for our business; she is a qualified line dance teacher and takes four line dance classes a week with her sister Pam. Preparation and practising also take up a lot of her time. I think line dancing is like the plague: once you have it, you never get rid of it. The amount of people involved is incredible. Everywhere you go, there is a hall that includes line dancing at some point in the week. I do not participate, but good luck to those who do.

We see our son and daughter and their families fairly regularly and are very proud of them all.

We are at the stage now where we are thinking of retirement; only one small problem – have a guess what that is!

PREFACE (Boxing)

I started working in the building industry some forty-four years ago and have stayed there. This will no doubt have people wondering how I still have a brain left to write about my laughter, grief, happiness, terror, and all the other feelings people have in life. It is because of all the incredible situations I have been in – often situations of my own making.

I started work at fifteen years of age, and my only love at that time was boxing. I had started at as a nine-year-old and had my first bout when I was eleven. I boxed a boy who was also eleven years old named D Hawkins from Alton. I won on points, (as opposed to a knockout). I went on to box for England as an amateur. I turned professional at twenty years of age, had twenty professional fights and won fifteen. I went to South Africa and beat a boxer called Kozey Smith over ten rounds. In his next fight he became the South African champion. I jumped to number eight in the world rankings, but my glory days were short-lived, I suffered a serious elbow injury which eventually forced me to retire from boxing, a sport I still love.

This book is mainly about some of the experiences I encountered in the building industry, but I must tell you one story about a laugh we had in South Africa.

I said 'we' as I was one of three: myself, former British middleweight champion Les Macateer, and his manager, Johnny Campbell. Johnny was to look after me, and while I was there he did a great job. He and Les were good blokes; it was a pleasure knowing them.

We were there for ten days before the fights and about four days after. The promoter Harry Levin asked me if we would like to go and see Mike and Bernie Winters at the theatre. I said I would ask the others, and of course the answer was yes.

When Mr Levin came and gave me the tickets, he said that in South Africa it was important to wear a shirt, tie, and smart trousers. There was no TV at the time, only radio. Going out to sports venues and the theatre, and so forth involved being properly dressed. I said we would all come 'properly dressed'. I told the others we had to wear a shirt and smart trousers; I 'forgot' the tie. On the night we chose to walk, as the theatre was only a mile away. I dressed as the others had, according to my incomplete instructions. I had three ties in my pocket. I also had the tickets, and, when we reached the theatre, I went to the foyer and gave the lady the tickets. She asked why we were not wearing ties. I said that we were British and knew nothing about this; the others also said that they were very surprised, but when we looked around, every man was wearing a tie. We said we would have to hurry back to the hotel and hopefully return to the theatre before the start of the show. After about one hundred yards of running, I told Johnny and Les that I had three ties in my pocket and that I knew about the rule the whole time.

For the next few minutes I was given renditions of Scots (Johnny) and Scouse (Les) swear words, some of which I had never heard before. (I expect I had, but I couldn't decipher the 'Northern and Scots' terminology. We were soon mates again, and the show was great. After we left for home, our paths never crossed again, but I will never forget them; they were great blokes.

CHAPTER ONE

I will start by telling of my apprenticeship as a carpenter, this in itself being debatable.

Having left school and begun seeking a job, I was advised by a School Counsellor to become an electrician. My dad then advised me to become a plumber, which provided more money even in those days., and my trainer (I was a very keen athlete at the time) said his building company did not have any plumbing vacancies, only one for a carpenter. Hence after an initial interview I became a carpenter, working for a company employing approximately 100 people, a very large firm in those days. The wages were very poor; I remember fully skilled tradesmen saying that they took home about 13 pounds, 10 shillings for a 52 ½-hour week. However, we were, generally speaking, a very happy bunch of blokes.

In the last few years it has become much harder to get quality labour, both labourers and tradesmen. When apprenticeships 'died,' it was a truly sad day for the building industry. Everyone had to have instant, ready-made tradesmen. This resulted in sky-high costs, particularly from plumbers, who seem to be able to charge what they like. I know of one plumber who charges £400 per day, and a carpenter £200 per day. This cannot go on, can it? Bring back government-sponsored apprenticeships as soon as possible.

In my first job mentioned above, one of the foremen, Tom, thought that the word f— was in the English Concise Dictionary hall of fame; it was his most popular word. Being just fifteen and not worldly wise, and hearing this giant of a man use the f— word so well was quite an experience! It certainly ensured that all the apprentices did exactly as they were told.

Tea break and lunchtime we sat in a large shed with planks on building blocks as seats and the new boy, me, was made to sit by the door, which was always open, whatever the weather. The first day, after being told where to sit, I found out within seconds why. Tom ate vast amounts of sandwiches during the day. However, he did not like the crust of the bread, which meant he took off the crusts and hurled them out the door, not aiming at all. Not only did he have a twisted sense of humour, he had a bent arm, resulting in target two, me, getting bread crusts implanted on all areas of the body. This of course was hilarious to the others, which resulted in Tom throwing more and more bread my way and turning the f— word into poetry. This only lasted a few weeks; I was soon sent back to the yard where the joiner's shop was because the apprenticeship was for carpentry and joinery. This was much better – indoors and I got to learn my trade with people who had more than one word in their arsenal.

CHAPTER 2

The joiner's shop was at the top of a large building, with the machine shop at ground level. Arthur, the yard manager was a war veteran who had his left leg amputated below the knee after a hand grenade was thrown at his patrol in the Far East. He survived because, although his injury was serious and gangrenous, maggots ate the gangrene and saved his life. I think he was Tom's ex-apprentice in speech therapy; he, too, loved the f— word. I must say that despite the language, all the blokes that I met at the firm were decent and kind people and would help you whenever they could.

My apprenticeship included day-release, and I went to Guildford Technical College for three and a half years, passed my city and guilds exams, and made friends with lots of fellow chippies.

On return from our summer break one year, one of the other students (Mark) did not show up. Not much was said, but after two more weeks of absence we asked a teacher where he was. He said he had just received a letter from Mark's firm saying that he had died of leukaemia. We were all shocked. He had not told us that he was ill. To this day, I think of him regularly; he was a really nice bloke. I finished my apprenticeship, and two years later, I left the firm and went elsewhere to a firm in Aldershot. I met a chap called Tony and shortly afterwards went with him to a firm near Reading where they were paying ten shillings an hour, a near fortune in those days.

We stayed there for about four months then started work for a firm which carried out work in army camps. We were given a costing book and knew exactly how much we earned. It was all written down and easy to understand. Our first job was to build a huge storage area in a big shed. All the storage rooms were made up of 4 × 2 partitions, with wire mesh ceilings.

This should have been an easy task for us, but it was complicated by the addition of Tony's new partner. Tony had a new dog, untrained in all departments and capable of running at great speed. Tony, in between working, was training the dog to sit, stand, lie, and so on, to no great success. The dog loved running, and, over the few weeks, it showed Tony how to chase him around the shed before crashing out knackered (Tony, that is, not the dog). This could not last; the dog was far fitter, and he was eventually left at home with Tony's wife.

We both left this firm and started private work carpentry and building. At first it was only small jobs, but we were very busy. My dad was not happy where he was working, and with our work load, he was able to come work with Tony and myself. Unfortunately three became a crowd, and we split up when Tony left.

CHAPTER 3

The two of us, father and son, started a building firm, which, nearly forty years later, still exists. We did a variety of jobs, and met nice, reasonable people and some not so nice people along the way. There are people whose feet do not touch the ground. For example, we were once asked to price a job of concreting a small area at the rear of a large house. The lady I met at the house was foreign and was the financial advisor to the owner. She showed me what was required – a new concrete area to stop trades people slipping on the existing concrete. After we'd priced the job, she rang to say what an exorbitant sum I was charging for concreting an area the size of a handkerchief. I returned and was told to make good the existing concrete where required rather than pour a new concrete area. I priced the job at £36, and it was accepted. We did the job within a few days, mixing ballast, sharp sand, and cement, making good where required. 'Thundernuts' (as we called the financial advisor) appeared on a regular basis, ensuring all was to her satisfaction. We were soon fed up with this, and, after a small meeting, the next time she appeared, we asked her if the kettle was boiling in the kitchen, hoping to have a break from her for a while. Thundernuts' was incredibly agile; her head turned round without the rest of her body moving, and she catapulted into the kitchen, instantly returning to say the kettle was not on. Her moaning about the project never stopped, and after we had gone, my father and I both thought we would never be paid. The cheque was sent by return of post. We knew we had her 'sussed'.

Another time, we built a large extension to a house in a small village call Crondall along with carrying out extensive alterations. The work entailed installing a new sceptic tank, as there was no main sewer in the area. We had to excavate a hole approximately 4 ½ metres long and wide × 4 metres deep, lay a concrete base, install a 3,000 gallon tank, fill the tank with water, cover it with concrete, and back-fill. This we did and here lies another story.

The Hy-Mak driver rang to say the he would be a day late. No problem for us; we had lots to do there. He came the following day, dug the hole as described, back-filled the hole, laid concrete, watched the tank fill with water. He told us that the previous job was identical to ours, except that the builder told the driver he was not going to fill the tank with water. He wanted the Hy-Mak placed over the tank overnight to stop the tank lifting through 'buoyancy'. The manufacturer's rep had told us to have the tank at least half-filled with water to stop the tank 'floating' until the concrete was hard, which we did. The Hy-Mak driver did as the builder asked (not the rep) and showed up the next morning to see the Hy-Mak and the tank two metres up in the air. It took another day to get the job done properly. We were glad that we had listened to the rep and done as he told us.

CHAPTER 4

We carried out a large job entailing remedial and repair work to a house in a Headley, Near Bordon. We had a long list of jobs to do in order of priority. Day one entailed delivery of tools and materials to site, but, on arrival, I discovered that I had left the house keys behind. Instead of going home and back again, we decided to take out the back door and frame, which had to be bricked up anyway, to save time and money and get the job going. This we did – broke the backdoor and frame and brought all our gear in. After toothing out some of the brickwork, we left the job for the plumbers to see. The plumbers, a father and son firm, had been working there the previous week and had a lot of equipment and materials there. When they arrived, they naturally wanted to know what had happened to the back door. We had made quite a mess and left it there and told them that someone had broken in over the weekend. They quickly raced upstairs to find that none of the gear had been taken, but were not happy with the situation. They asked what to do, and I suggested that they phone the police. Great idea. I then had a pretend conversation with the police while the plumbers listened in on what they thought was my half of the conversation. After I had finished, I told everyone that the CID were on their way. The plumbers were very impressed. CID – great stuff. By the time 3 p.m. came, they were pretty much fed up with the lack of police presence. When we told them the truth, the air was blue. It took a long time for them to forgive us; I wonder why.

CHAPTER 5

During the middle to late sixties we were incredibly busy. 'Gazumping' was at a high: people were buying, refurbishing. and selling at a nice profit, with plenty of people outbidding each other to get the property. We saw people crying outside the property belonging to someone else with a bigger pocket and a woman crying because she could not afford to do all the work required. May those days never return.

We carried out a job in Farnham– repairs to windows to a very large house with an orchard. We were with two painters, Harold and Jack, whom we knew very well. After a couple hours work, the lady of the house asked us if we would like tea. 'Thank you,' we answered. Whilst waiting in the conservatory, we talked about the fact that all the apples on the trees were wrapped in polythene and elastic bands to protect them from birds and insects. Dad and I by chance were near the conservatory door, which would turn out to be very handy. After beginning to drink the tea, we noticed the brown scum that is left behind when cups have not been washed properly. Dad and I threw our tea outside; but we could not tell Harold or Jack without being overheard, and they both drank theirs. When the lady asked if we would like some more tea, Dad and I both said 'yes, please'. Harold and Jack were in deep shock and each had to drink another cup of 'slop', as they later called it. Dad and I were hysterical, knowing we could dispose of our 'slop' quite easily.

Another time, my dad caught me out instead. I was usually the one who did the estimating for jobs, and one day Dad got someone to call me to estimate some carpentry work to be carried out. After one full hour of looking for a house that did not exist, I gave up. The following morning I was the joke of the day, but not for long. After a few weeks we, Harold, Bob, and myself, got a mate to call Dad regarding an estimate. Dad knew the bloke and made his own arrangements for the visit as I was on holiday. When I got back, I asked Dad how he had managed, only to be insulted with a tirade of royal blue language. We never 'did' each other again, not big time anyway.

We once carried out a conversion near Farnham, turning stables into a liveable house. At this time my dad and I were both into growing vegetables in pots, then transplanting them into the ground. On the way out of the drive one night, we stopped and looked at a gate that was in a boundary wall. We went in and within two metres on the right was a greenhouse filled with pots, all shapes and sizes. We arranged to 'attack' the greenhouse the following evening. We finished work a half-hour early, parked the van near the gate, went in without looking around, and helped ourselves to some of the pots. We turned around to see the back end of an eight-foot-tall stallion going out of the gate. We put back the pots in a panic. The stallion luckily had made his way down the drive, so I followed him. He then started to trot towards the big house with me in full sprint chasing behind. He went all the way round the house and back up the drive, where Dad was standing with a shovel in his hand. As the horse approached Dad, he said if I stopped chasing he would direct the horse back through the gate. Great idea. The horse made his way towards Dad, who, instead of directing the stallion the right direction through the gate, let him pass up the drive and onto the road. We spent the next two hours chasing 'Red Rum' up and down the road, in and out of house drives, until he decided that he had had enough fun for one day and allowed us to grab his rein and lead him back into the field. We were shattered, late, and pot-less.

CHAPTER 6

One of the funniest things that happened was also at a job in Farnham. We were replacing windows, and the lady of the house told us that she had a 'small' drink problem, which she was trying to cure.

One day we were asked in to have tea and were shown to the lounge where we sat. The lady disappeared; we sat talking for a while when a small voice saying 'Peep Bo' came from across the room. We looked at each other, then around the room, but saw no-one. Seconds later a further rendition of 'Peep Bo' was said from behind us. We stood up and made our way across the room to the bar area to see the lady sitting on the floor with a bottle of wine in one hand and a glass in the other. The three of us burst out laughing, and, despite our offer to help her up, she refused and we left her there. We never saw her in that state again, thank goodness.

I saw her many years later in hospital when visiting my mum. Her husband was very ill, but she found time to come and say hello and told me that she still remembered the incident above. She had kicked the habit and did not drink anymore. I often wondered if her last drink was after said incident.

CHAPTER 7

Without doubt, the most embarrassing moments of our working lives happened next door to an extension we were building in a village just outside Farnham. The people next door had a daughter, Mary, who was learning to play the piano. Every day when she returned home from school, she started playing, mostly Chopin (so we were told by her dad). She was brilliant and she was still learning. We made the never-to-be-forgotten mistake of complimenting her playing to her dad one day, who immediately asked if we would like to hear her play the piano. We could hardly say no, and we arranged to go next door the following afternoon. Mary's dad gave us the cue to enter, and we followed him to the lounge where we met his wife and sat down on a dust-sheet covered settee. There we were in our boots, jeans, and pencils behind our ears, waiting for Mary to appear. When she came in, Mum and Dad stood up, followed very elegantly, I must say, by us. Mary sat on her stool and said she would play Chopin minor or something in A major or, well, you get the idea. For the next fifteen minutes we sat there trying not to burst out laughing, and we were truly grateful when it was over. We congratulated Mary on her playing; even two dipsticks like us knew that she had a truly great talent. Looking back, I'm grateful for such nice people to have shared their obvious pride and love in their daughter. We never heard if she ever reached her objectives.

CHAPTER 8

Laughing at someone with an affliction is disgraceful, unless that person works in the building trade and should not be at work in the first place. One such instance was on a job that we were working on at Chawton, near Alton. We were carrying out a large refurbishment, and when our tea break or lunch was due, we sat in the garage. There were four of us, myself and my mate and a father and son bricklaying team. Jim, the father, had fallen over some months previous, and, although he was back at work, he had a limp where he had damaged his leg in the accident. The garage had a slope up to it, and Jim went to collect his lunch bag and came and sat in the garage. After lunch we got up and Jim, a tall and large man, went to put his lunch bag in his van about forty yards away. The slope was quite acute, and Jim, after starting to walk, realised he had no control over his walking speed. His bad leg was like a pendulum: once it started, it wouldn't stop. He couldn't control the other leg either, and he was in a hopeless situation unable to stop. His legs were moving at quite a speed, and he shouted for help just before he crashed into the back of the van. We had watched Jim for the last few moments of his journey, too far away to help him. We were in stitches at an out-of-control person crashing into his van. The damage to Jim and the van was almost nothing; only his ego was hurt. He did not come back to work for about four days though, until his leg was better. He has never been allowed to forget this incident.

Another time we had had some bother with a customer over the cost of a bill, and, after we had contacted a solicitor, it was agreed we would all meet at the customer's house and hopefully resolve the problem. We arrived early and waited outside for our solicitor to arrive. After a few minutes his car arrived with two people in it: our solicitor and our customer's solicitor. Talk about saving petrol, was this ethical? Was this legal? We never asked. The problem was resolved that day. We did not feel that everything was right, but what could we do?

CHAPTER 9

One time we had to replace some broken tiles on a house at Headley. No sooner were we up on the ladder when we were attacked by wasps, which had found a hole in the fascia board. We told the customer to put some powder around the hole in the evening when the wasps had settled, and we could come back the next day. We checked that he would be OK on a ladder, and he said he already had some powder.

The next day when we went back, we asked if everything had been done.
'Oh yes,' he said, you had better ask my wife; she went up there.

Talking about roofs, we had to go and collect some materials and told the roof tilers we would be about one hour. As the tilers were working on the chimney, they said that they would do some 'pointing in' for us. (This is filling in with cement between the bricks). They had a ladder which went from the ground right up to the top of the chimney, which was about ten feet above the bungalow roof. As we left, one of the tilers was climbing up the ladder. As we drove along we could see the chimney moving as the tiler climbed the ladder. We stopped and started sending hand messages, telling him the problem. He though we were taking the mickey and started waving his hands, making the chimney move even more. Fortunately his mate saw what was happening and got him to come down. Our hearts had been in our mouths, but no damage was done.

On another job I went to give an estimate to a customer who had a three-story house, including rooms in the roof, each with dormer windows. He took me outside and showed me a dormer window with tiles broken to both sides. Below this window was a conservatory with a glass roof, and I told him that scaffold was needed as it would be impossible to get a ladder long enough to reach.

The client suggested it might be possible to get out of the window, hang on to the window with one hand, move over to the corner of the dormer, and have someone inside pass me the tiles, which I could fit one-handed. After a few seconds thought, I suggested that he contacted a zoo to see if they had a long-armed orang-utan for hire that could do a small roof repair job. I walked away and drove off. I never heard from him again. Thank you!

CHAPTER 10

Over the years we have worked for a lot of really lovely people; most people are deep down and none more so than a Sir and Lady 'Smith', who have now passed away. We used to do the maintenance on a very large house, which had been turned into five large flats. Sir and Lady Smith lived in one flat, and we were often called out to do minor jobs and repairs. One day I was asked to go and repair a lock and turned up to find the flat empty. I waited and after about ten minutes they appeared, having been out with the dog. They waved me to go in, which I did with my tools, to be followed by Sir Smith, who told me 'never to do that again'. I asked him what he meant, and he said that whenever I was working for them I must treat the house as my own and come and go as I pleased. Coming from a titled person, I was slightly embarrassed but knew that he really meant what he said.

The lady who cleaned for Sir and Lady Smith lived about one mile from their flat; she refused the Smiths' offers of a lift, and, despite being in her seventies, walked there three times a week. We got to know this lady, and she wanted some work done in her kitchen. I gave her a price, which she accepted, and we did the work. What she had not told us was that she owned a pony-sized Alsatian dog who did not like visitors. While we worked in the kitchen, the dog was locked up in the sitting room. We had no reason to go in there, trust me. One day, Dad went to the van to get some tools while I was outside doing a small job. The lady had gone up the garden, leaving the window in the lounge open. The dog, hearing the kitchen door slam, got out of the window and sprinted down the path towards Dad. By chance he had a container in his hands to put the tools in and as the dog jumped at him, he was able to place the container over the dog's head. The old lady heard the barking of the dog and the squeal of Dad and called the dog back. Dad was not hurt, just paralysed, and I cannot repeat his opinion of the dog and what the lady should do with it.

Sir Smith died first, and Lady Smith lived on her own for several years. During this time she suffered senile dementia, and one day someone knocked on her door, talked his way in, and offered her peanut money for her furniture. She accepted and he walked away, having made a huge profit. This happened on several occasions, and the other residents got to hear of what was happening. They informed the police, who told them that the man had done nothing illegal. If he made an offer for anything she owned and she accepted, it was legal. They did say, however, that if it happened again to give them a call and they would have a word in his ear. He was never seen again. Was he told? We will never know. Lady Smith went into a home, where she eventually passed away.

CHAPTER 11

Another time we had an encounter with a dog was when we did a refurbishment at a Police station involving taking out existing kitchens to three houses and fitting new ones. The middle house occupant had a pet Alsatian, which, like the previous dog, did not like visitors. He was put in the next room and did not have any contact with us until one day I went out to get some materials which were lying by the hedge. The policeman had been out in his car and came back just as I was about to pick up the materials. He opened the back door, and the dog made a beeline for me and jumped up at my throat. I fell back in the hedge and the dog just missed my throat, but marked my chest. Thankfully it was just that, a mark.

The policeman called the dog back and told me how lucky I was and walked in, no apology necessary, he obviously thought. He and one of the other policemen were thrown out of the force about two years later. They had swapped wives.

About two weeks after the above incident, another officer came and asked if I could give him a price for some work. Upon arrival at his house, which was on a large estate, I knocked on the front door, only to hear the back door open.

I walked down the path, round the corner, and was faced with another pony-sized Alsatian travelling at sixty miles per hour towards me. The pathetic squeal coming from me, did not stop him, and he jumped at me, placed his paws on my shoulder, and licked me to death. It is very difficult to describe total happiness, but believe me, I experienced it that evening when I realized I wasn't going to die. If there are any would-be inventors out there, a hand-held portable loo is desperately needed for people who, like myself, find themselves in those situations.

Alsations weren't the only animals that made work interesting. I have only ridden a horse once. One customer had several and asked if I would like to have a short ride. I was very keen at the time and accepted his offer. I dealt with measurements all the time, so I remember clearly that the horse was about eight feet tall, no joking. I am six feet tall. Without any carpentry experience, I'm sure you can do that math. It took three people to get me into the saddle, and off we went –me bouncing up when I should have been going down and vice versa. The result was one bruised backside. As I said, it only happened once, and that's the way it will remain.

CHAPTER 12

In 1988 we built a house for a lady and installed roof windows. She telephoned a few months ago that one of the windows had warped and would not open. The window was made by one of the biggest manufacturers and, on inspection, it looked as though it had been hit by something. The damage was to the opening sash, not the frame, and I telephoned the manufacturer only to be told that their windows had all been redesigned and would not fit the old window frame. We were left in limbo until we started a job locally, where I had fitted roof windows some twenty years ago. The customer wanted the roof windows taken out and dormer windows installed. Yes, they were the same sized windows. We bought one from one client and, in half an hour, installed it for another, saving hundreds of pounds. Good luck or what?

While we were building the house in 1988, which was on a small farm, we noticed six newly hatched ducks one day, each so tiny. The gate to the yard had been covered in wire so that the ducks could not get out, but somehow a small hole had appeared at the bottom of the wire. We were working on the roof, and someone looked down to see the baby ducks walking down the drive towards the road. The four of us raced down the ladder, and two of us stood in the road to stop any traffic, the other two chasing the ducks, who followed one leader in a snake-like order. It only took about five minutes to get them back inside, by which time there were two small queues of traffic. Most drivers had big smiles on their faces, as did the owner, who was very disappointed that he had not filmed four grown men taking so much trouble over six small ducklings.

CHAPTER 13

In 1998 my wife contracted breast cancer, which came as a horrendous blow to both of us. I was working at the time for a millionaire banker who lived in a manor house in the country. My wife had an operation within ten days of finding out, and I had a few days off afterwards to help out when she came home. I told my customer, who said that he understood and told me that he had bowel cancer. When I got back to work, me, with my working class roots, and the millionaire banker were able to talk on the same level simply because of the illnesses involved. My customer flew all over the world to try new drugs, but sadly died while we were working there, leaving a wife and children behind. I was very sorry when this man died. Who said money is everything? My wife has now made a full recovery. The treatment and service offered by the N.H.S. was second to none. I hope that she never has to go through that again. May a cure be found soon for everyone.

I saw an old mate in Farnham about two years after my wife had had her operation. He told me that his wife had contracted breast cancer, but despite having an operation, she died a few months later. On telling me this, he broke down and burst into tears. I consoled him as best I could, but what can you do? As I said before, someone, please find a cure.

CHAPTER 14

My wife and I were lucky enough to have some money to buy a boat, which we moored on the Thames at Walton. It was a thirty-three-foot Dawncraft, and it slept four easily, so our son, daughter, and friends were able to come and stay over on the boat at weekends. There is not enough paper in London to write about all the laughter we enjoyed and near disasters we endured. I will tell a few stories though.

We bought our first boat privately at Kingston, a sixteen-foot open boat with a small engine and a trailer. The trailer had only two wheels, which meant that when you reversed you had to have an opposite lock on the steering wheel to go the way that you wanted down the slipway. I had never done this before, and it caused chaos when dozens of car owners were watching this lunatic going up and down the ramp, across the road and back again. I was useless at reversing the trailer. We sold the boat.

We went to an auction at Egham Boat Yard and bought the Dawncraft previously mentioned. We spent some money on it to bring it up to par and found a mooring at Walton, right outside the Anchor Pub. We were amazed to discover that you do not have to have a lesson or exam on basic boat manoeuvres, steering, or mooring. You just buy a boat, get a river licence, and off you go. We were soon pretty good at steering, reversing, mooring and so forth, and we loved it. The Thames is a brilliant river and has very good facilities. We only stayed on the non-tidal part of the river; our boat and engine were not powerful enough to withstand tidal water. We pretty much did the same trip nearly every weekend when we went upriver to Staines, had a pub lunch, and then back home again.

On the way home one day there were just the two of us, and the river was flowing very fast. We had not experienced such strong currents before, and we missed our mooring when reaching The Anchor at Walton, so we turned round and tried to go upstream. The current had got worse, and we were hardly moving. I steered the boat to the edge of the bank and asked my wife to jump off with the front rope, and then we could pull the boat to the mooring. She said she could not jump off. I said jump! She said *no!* After a few terse words, she jumped right into a large clump of stinging nettles. She was not happy for a while. We managed to get back okay. My wife managing to jump when the boat was going at breakneck speed certainly helped!

After that, we always looked at the weather forecast before going out.

We took some friends out one weekend, enjoyed lunch, and then got back on board. I asked Terry to stay on the bank and push the front of the boat out, then come to the back and get aboard. He pushed the boat out, slipped, and grabbed the railing at the front of the boat, but his feet were stuck on the bank. His weight had pushed the boat out, and, if left, he would have grown six to nine inches in a very short period of time. I had a long boat hook, so I went to the front of the boat, grabbed a small clump of grass with it, and managed to pull the boat back to the bank. The journey home took a little longer than it should have, as we were all crying with laughter after the incident.

One week we went on a trip up the Thames; our intention was to reach Oxford. We did not get that far as our gear control wire had stretched and did not work properly. We stopped at the nearest boatyard, and they said that they could do the work; it would take about four hours, but they would have to get the parts from the local town. We agreed on a price and waited. They came and took the gear lever and parts and about three hours later came and put it together. We paid the boss, who suggested that we take the boat downriver to see it if was okay. If the cable needed adjustment, they would do this for us. We set off down the river and found the lever as useless as before. We went back, told the foreman, who went to the workshop to get some tools. He came back to tell us that the new mechanism was still in the workshop; they had taken off the old gear control, taken it inside, and left it for someone else to pick up and re-fix the new unit, unfortunately this had been overlooked. The staff at the firm had been really friendly, and we could only laugh at what at happened. We were soon on our way with our new gear control in place.

CHAPTER 15

Whilst this book is the story of my life in the building industry, I must tell the story of my drawing ability while at school. I went to Heath End Secondary Modern School, and one year our art teacher, a Mr Evens, told us our art exam would be that morning. Our subject was to be of a farming nature, and we were told to use our imaginations and draw a farmyard scene. I pondered for a few minutes and decided to draw a picture of a child lying on a path directly behind a chicken, with a farm worker a long way away working in the field. I took very great care to put everyone in proportion, and when the picture was finished I thought it looked great, for about ten seconds. I had not got my proportions right. The scene was horrendous: there was this tiny child lying under a truly massive chicken, which took up about two thirds of the picture. Also under the chicken was this tiny, tiny man holding a shovel. There was no perspective: the child, the farm worker, and the chicken were all standing on the same piece of land. The humans had shrunk to miniature status, and the chicken would have fed twenty people. Worse was to follow. We had to walk to the front of the class and let everyone see our masterpieces. Most of the drawings, as I remember, were quite good; then it was my turn. The class took one look at my picture and broke into uncontrollable laughter, even the teacher Mr Evans. How could they? Van Dyke did not have to put up with this, did he? I returned to my chair totally embarrassed. It did not last long though; soon I could see the funny side. I scored 40 per cent, the lowest pass mark, totally deserved for the funniest drawing in the class.

CHAPTER 16

Back to work.

We were building a small porch for a lady just outside Farnham, and one day it poured with rain. We stood in the garage waiting for the rain to stop when an elderly lady asked for directions to a certain house. I told her that I had never heard of it, and she said that she was looking for her nephew, Mark. There was a home nearby for children, and I suggested that this was perhaps where Mark was staying. I offered her a lift to the home, and she accepted. When we reached it, I explained the situation to a nurse and was told that the lady's nephew was not at the home. She suggested I take the lady to an old peoples' home near the hospital. When we got there, I told her to wait in the truck and found a nurse who was truly grateful that I had found and returned one of their fold. I accepted their thanks, forgetting to tell them that the lady had initially found me, and I was pointed in the right direction by someone else. What a gentleman!

Another incident took place on the same job.

Barry, my mate, had been looking to buy a caravan for some time, and the house next door had a caravan for sale in the drive. Barry stayed late one day to wait for the owners to come home and was told that he could have the caravan for £50. When he told me the next day, I asked him what was wrong with it. Who sells a caravan for £50? I must say the caravan looked in good condition, and after Barry had a friend look it over, he bought the caravan. He arranged to pick up the caravan the following Saturday morning, so I wished him luck for the weekend as we parted ways Friday evening. On Monday morning Barry was unusually late, and when he did arrive, his face gave away a recent disaster in his life. He explained how he had collected the caravan, driven it to Farnborough on his way home, come to a roundabout, and, after going about fifty feet around the roundabout, heard an almighty crash. He looked in the mirror to see no caravan. He stopped, of course, and when he got out, Barry found his caravan had disintegrated and was spread all over the road and part of the roundabout. He was in deep shock, and it took several minutes before he began to 'pick up the pieces'. The police came and took control, helped him put the remains on the roundabout, and, as no one had been hurt, he would not be charged with any offence. Apparently it took Barry all weekend to clear the rubbish, and everyone, including the police, had something to laugh about that weekend. What a sick society we live in.

CHAPTER 17

My Dad and I converted a large barn into living quarters, and an interesting couple lived next door. He was a city banker, and she, a huge lady, an African queen of a tribe from her homeland. She spoke perfect English, and we spoke to her nearly every day. She was a diamond.

The plumber showed up to do some work on the property and asked who had lit a fire next door. We told him that the lady next door was a tribal queen from Africa and every Thursday afternoon lit a fire and armed herself with suitable machete knives to drive away evil spirits from her tribe. The plumber did not believe one word of this at first, but after much persuasion by us, he finally accepted it as true. It was difficult to keep a straight face after convincing someone of such rubbish, but we managed it. We did tell him the truth some time later; he was not amused, and who could blame him? We told the lady next door what we had done, and she laughed as we had. Tribal ritual my foot!

We did a small roof alteration near Aldershot. One day I went to get some materials and came back about one hour late for lunch. I had bought fish and chips for my lunch and asked the lady if she would mind putting the fish and chips in the oven while we moved the materials from the truck. When we had finished unloading, I asked for the bag and she told me it was in the kitchen. She had brought in a small table with plate, knife, fork, and spoon etc., and said that I was to eat in, with a sweet to follow. I really appreciated her generosity; not many people would go to such trouble.

We built a very large extension for a couple near Farnborough. Bill was a scientist at the R.A.E, a real diamond of a man. While the work was being done, he came home every lunch time to make sure everything was okay. We had to dig the footing by hand as there was no room for a digger. After two to three days we called the building inspector to inspect the footings, and everything was fine. We had to knock up the concrete by hand (mixer), and we were waiting for the ballast and cement to come when Bill came home for lunch. He examined the trenches and asked if everything was okay. We said everything was fine and that the bricklayers were coming the next day. Bill asked how we were going to get the concrete finished that day and get the bricks and blocks in such a short space of time. We said the base of the foundation was down to the level of the house footings, and we would build directly on the soil. Bill, poor sod, went into shock, looking like a man in desperate need of oxygen. The look on his face made us burst into laughter; he then realised that he had been turned over. He should have known us by then, but we caught him again when we reached roof level. The bricklayer had bedded the roof plates, cleaned up, and gone. We were literally waiting for the roof timbers to come when Bill came home for an early lunch. We were making our way down the ladder when he came round and asked us how things were going. We said that everything was fine, the roof was ready to be cut, we were really grateful for the way that we had been looked after, and we wished him and his wife all the best in finishing the extension. For the second time, Bill looked to us like he was going to have a heart attack Then he noticed us crying with laughter. I do not know whether scientists swore in those days; Bill certainly did not, but he did have a good reason.

CHAPTER 18

We built an extension for an estate agent's home once, which included building a bathroom. When it came to fitting out the bathroom, the lady told us exactly what she wanted, and we ordered the suite as directed. When it came, we laid out the suite as required and waited for the gentleman to offer his opinion. The suite included a bidet, something he had obviously not seen before. As soon as he saw it, he asked his wife what it was. We walked away when we heard him ask; his wife went beetroot red and said that it was for washing their feet. He observed that it was the most expensive foot wash that he had ever seen. Well it was, wasn't it! We never did find out when he was told what it was actually for. Everyone knows it's for cleaning your teeth, isn't it?

Most of the people that you meet in life are decent, honest people. The building industry included. You also meet some strange characters. One, a painter, showed up on his first day at our firm wearing a shirt, tie, flannel trousers, sports coat, and hat. We thought that he was the architect. His wife, apparently, was a proud lady and refused to let her neighbours know that she was married to a painter.

I have a cousin who used to drive a lorry with his brother, the two of them delivering sand, ballast and so forth. He had the job of cutting the edge of a bank, which had overgrown onto the road. He put the waste grass and soil into a digger bucket and then into the lorry. A house owner came over and told my cousin not to take too much of the bank away, as he would soon be on his property. He continued to question my cousin to make sure Tom knew what he was doing. Tom assured the gentlemen that he knew what he was doing. The gentleman was not reassured and continued informing Tom that he wanted a perfect job. After several minutes of listening to the man's requirements, Tom had had enough, picked up the man, laid him in the digger bucket and lifted the bucket up to its full height. He carried on working until the man apologised, then he let him down. There were no more instructions given that day.

CHAPTER 19

I have worked with some first class tradesmen, none more so than a carpenter called Bert. He was an elderly bloke when I started work, and he and his son worked together. We became friends, and I was invited to both their homes on different occasions. When I went to Bert's house, he showed me his finest piece of work, a chain of about eight links made from a solid piece of mahogany. The links were very smooth; it was brilliant.

I have also seen shabby workmanship, none more so than a job that I visited recently. A woman wanted all her doors changed beginning with the first floor. She got a carpenter to hang the doors, which were six panelled compressed hardboard doors. There was a difference of opinion about the money, and she only had him hang the upstairs doors. She gave me a call to price the downstairs doors, and I went round to be told the story. As I was about to leave, she asked if I would perhaps like to see his workmanship as she did not think that they had been hung well. She was right: he had hung them all upside down, with the large rail at the top. She was furious; he had already been paid.

CHAPTER 20

The lack of communication in the building industry is world class. The authorities concerned sometimes leave everyone ignorant of the most basic information required.

We did a job in the town converting two shops into three flats. The shops, many years ago, had been houses, yet changing use from shops to living quarters entailed eighteen groups of people having the right to object to change of use. It took the owner over a year to get permission. The biggest problem, from their points of view, was the fact that the properties were listed buildings. That part out of the way, I gave the owner a quote, which was accepted. We agreed on a starting date, and the work began. When I say the work began, it began for about six hours, at which point the listed building officer from the council showed up to tell us that we had to stop work, as some of the oak beams shown on the plan were to be covered with plasterboard, which was not acceptable to him. Until this problem was resolved, he said, work was to stop. I telephoned the local authority and asked the building inspector for a visit. He said that the beams had to be covered because of fire regulations if there were to be flats above. I asked if he could meet the listed building office and discuss a compromise; he pointed out that he and the listed building office did not like each other, did not speak to each other, and only communicated by letter. I told the owner the story, and she was mortified. What could be done? To cut a long story short, I left the job for one week, wrote to the building inspector and the listed building inspector to tell them I was starting the project again, and the problem over the beams would have to be discussed further. We never saw the listed building inspector, and the job went along quite smoothly. How difficult this could have become! The council concerning the listed building inspector and building control, in my view, was a shambles.

While we were working on that same job, I met with the owner's husband on a Saturday morning to discuss the work. I arrived to find him knocking a brick pier down. A pier is a brick or blockwork structure built into a wall for strength. I do not know many people who knock a wall down by starting at the bottom, but he did. As he was taking the brickwork down, the loose bricks above were falling down to the ground floor. After seeing what was happening, when the next bricks fell down, I shouted, 'Stop! I've been hit by a brick!' He did not even know that I was there, and hearing me shouting that I had been hit by a brick sent him charging down the stairs wondering how badly hurt I was. When he saw me standing there with a big grin on my face, relief and anger took over. I think that I can honestly say he called me all the names in the book. We had known each other for many years and were soon laughing at the incident. The job went well, and the owner sold the flats very quickly. Amazingly, the flats are still there, not having been changed into anything else yet.

Still on the topic of communication, I do not think that it is possible to overstress how important it is for the builder and the customer to know exactly what the builder has allowed for in his estimate and what the customer thinks that he or she will be getting. This is very important when an extension to a property is required, there are so many grey areas in play. Has the builder allowed a deep enough foundation for the extension, will the bricks be the same, are the roof tiles to be the same, and so on.

Most of these questions are stipulated on the plan and laid out by the architect. However, foundations for extensions will almost certainly have to go down to the same depth as the house or bungalow involved. Does the builder know this? Does the owner know? Almost certainly, the answer to both questions is no. The locality of bushes, shrubs, and trees grown since the original property was built may well mean the foundations for the extension will have to be deeper than the original foundations simply because roots of trees have grown deeper. For this reason, all of my estimates include the foundation depth needed for the extension. This allows the builder to work out the exact amount of concrete and underground brick and blockwork required. Building control at the local authority are normally very helpful and, in a lot of cases, would be able to tell the builder and customer how deep the foundations will have to be, allowing for any tree root, or shrubs in the new footings area.

The points I have just made may seem obvious, but they are not in all cases. Once the foundations have been built, the brick and blockwork built to damp course, and the trench back-filled, it is impossible to know how deep the footings are. I have built extensions where the footings have been one, two, and three metres deep, but once the ground has been levelled off, who knows? Not sorting out the depth of footings can lead to arguments over thousands of pounds; excavation and concrete are expensive. It is doubtful that many people who have extensions and alteration work carried out have any knowledge whatsoever about the building industry and, in most cases, should seek advice, possibly from the architect as to where to get estimates from. I would suggest you get a building company of experience; they may not be the cheapest, but good workmanship is not cheap.

CHAPTER 21

I rent a small yard, and some years ago the owners wanted a new shower/bathroom suite. I gave them an estimate and they accepted it.

I included a separate sum of money to supply and fit the glazed tiling. They were not sure how much tiling they wanted until the suite was in position. When we had fitted the shower/bathroom suite, they decided to have a considerable amount of tiling, much more than I had allowed for in my estimate. I did not tell my customers that the tiling was going to be a lot more money, thinking they realized this. We bought the tiles, fitted them as required, and our job was done. When I sent the bill, I got a telephone call from the owner in which he accused me of being a thief and con man. I tried to explain that this was certainly not the case; the only mistake I had made was not keeping them informed of the exact cost of the extra tiling. They reluctantly paid the bill in full, but it was many weeks before we were talking on friendly terms again. This little story taught me that you can never give the customer too much information, particularly when it means they have to stump up more money. They say money is the root of all evil. Well, it is also the root of a lot of good. We have to reach a point where we explain things to each other, so we can have a lot less grief over it.

CHAPTER 22

We did some sub-contract work for a builder mate at Cranleigh near Guildford. It was a large contract, and we were there for about two months.

The job entailed a new spiral staircase from the cellar up to the first floor landing. The holes had been cut into the joists to accept the staircase and floorboards, and ladders were put in for easy movement to whichever level you required. One of the ladders always had a little bit of movement, but after a while we got used to that. The owners used to come down and visit the house every Friday afternoon to see the progress of the work and to talk to the builder.

One particular Friday we were taking our tools to the van and I was up and down the ladder. I came down the wobbly ladder with a bag of tools, and when it moved, I slipped, dropped the tools, and had to jump down to the planks below. I was not hurt, just shaken, but the tools were everywhere. I called the ladder, the planks, and everyone and everything that existed all the names I had learnt over the years and then some. I then came up to ground level to see the owners with their son and daughter talking to the builder about ten yards away. Embarrassment was not the word; where could I go? Disappear? I waited for the conversation to finish and went over and apologised for my language, expecting my removal from the job at least. The owners said they had heard nothing, and even if they had, it was no worse than they themselves used. Their diplomacy was first class; everyone in the whole house had heard me. I was very grateful for their tact; they could very easily have made an issue over that and had me thrown out.

CHAPTER 23

We bought a plot of land in the early eighties with a view to making a nice profit. No chance – interest rates were 12 per cent when we bought the plot. After seven months, which was the time it took to build the house and sell it, interest rates were 15 per cent. We were paying 3 per cent over the top, and the house was not a money spinner; we just about covered our costs.

When we began to connect the sewer, the route shown on the plan was available to us; so we contacted the building inspector, who told us that we would have to connect to the sewer in the road, five metres down. He said that he would send a road engineer to give us some advice. He came that day, gave us the information required, and was about to leave when we asked whether we needed to give the public any notice about closing the narrow road outside the house, as we had heard that it was usually two weeks notice. He said that was normally the case, but as it was him, and as we were in a hurry to get the job done, he said to put the bollards up and shut the road. We were to call him when we were ready to make the connection. This we did. We closed the road, put up bollards and safety rails, and away we went. Within one hour, a very posh lady came along and asked why we had not given notice to the public regarding shutting the road. We apologised and told her the builder had gone abroad; he always did when there were problems. She then wanted to know his name. As if. We said we could not disclose his name; it was worth more than our jobs if we did. She then told us that her husband was a road engineer and she would find out what action she could take, as she and everyone else could not drive along that stretch of road. What had we done? We'd told this woman a lot of tripe, thinking it was funny, and now we were for the high jump. We did the connection and back-filled the hole in the road in about three days. Everything went well, but every hour of every day we were expecting the council or the police, or both, to come and take us away, lock us up, and throw away the key. Disaster, perhaps even the finish of our firm? Nothing happened. I do not know if we were lucky or the woman decided not to follow up. As I have previously said, communication is so important between the public and builders, which goes to show just how hypocritical can I be. In the end, I suppose we all teach ourselves our very own lessons.